THE AFFILIATE MARKETING REVOLUTION

An Ironclad Blueprint for Results

Chloe Fairchild

C O N T E N T S

CHAPTER 1

INTRODUCTION TO AFFILIATE MARKETING

Affiliate marketing has come a long way since its inception in the 1990s. It started with Amazon's Associate Program, which allowed website owners to promote products and earn commissions. Today, it has evolved into a multi-billion-dollar industry with various types of affiliate programs and networks.

Why Affiliate Marketing?

Affiliate marketing offers several benefits, such as low start-up costs, passive income generation, and scalability. By promoting other companies' products or services, you can earn commissions without worrying about inventory, shipping, or customer support.

What is Affiliate Marketing?

Affiliate marketing is a performance-based marketing strategy where individuals or businesses promote products or services of other companies and earn a commission for each sale or lead generated through their efforts. It is a mutually beneficial arrangement where affiliates help drive sales and businesses gain exposure and customers.

How Does Affiliate Marketing Work?

Affiliate marketing involves three main parties: the merchant (seller), the affiliate (promoter), and the customer. The process typically follows these steps:

1. The merchant creates an affiliate program and provides unique affiliate links or promo codes to the affiliates.

2. Affiliates promote the merchant's products or services through various marketing channels such as websites, blogs, social media, email marketing, or paid advertising.

3. When a customer clicks on the affiliate's link or uses their promo code to make a purchase, the affiliate's unique identifier is tracked by the merchant's affiliate tracking system.

4. The merchant verifies the sale or lead generated by the affiliate and pays them a commission based on the agreed-upon terms.

5. The customer receives the product or service they purchased, and the merchant handles customer support and order fulfillment.

Benefits of Affiliate Marketing

Affiliate marketing offers several benefits for both merchants and affiliates:

1. Low Risk: Merchants only pay affiliates when they generate a sale or lead, making it a cost-effective marketing strategy.

2. Increased Reach: Affiliates can promote products or services to a wider audience, leveraging their existing online presence and networks.

3. Diverse Marketing Channels: Affiliates can use various marketing channels to promote products, including websites, blogs, social media, email marketing, and more.

4. Passive Income Potential: Once affiliates set up their promotional campaigns, they can earn passive income as long as their links continue to generate sales or leads.

5. Performance-Based: Affiliates are motivated to drive results as their earnings depend on their performance, leading to a win-win situation for both parties.

Types of Affiliate Marketing

There are different types of affiliate marketing models, including:

1. Pay-Per-Sale (PPS): Affiliates earn a commission for each sale they generate through their referral link.

2. Pay-Per-Lead (PPL): Affiliates earn a commission for each lead they generate, such as a sign-up or form submission.

3. Pay-Per-Click (PPC): Affiliates earn a commission for each click on their affiliate link, regardless of whether a sale or lead is generated.

4. Pay-Per-Call (PPC): Affiliates earn a commission for each phone call generated through their promotional efforts.

Affiliate Marketing Networks

Affiliate marketing networks act as intermediaries between merchants and affiliates, providing a platform for affiliates to find suitable affiliate programs and track their earnings. Some popular affiliate marketing networks include:

1. Amazon Associates

2. ClickBank

3. Commission Junction (CJ Affiliate)

4. ShareASale

5. Rakuten Advertising (formerly LinkShare)

Getting Started with Affiliate Marketing

To get started with affiliate marketing, follow these steps:

1. Choose a niche: Select a specific industry or topic that aligns with your interests and expertise.

2. Research affiliate programs: Find affiliate programs that offer products or services related to your chosen niche.

3. Join affiliate networks: Sign up for affiliate networks to access a wide range of affiliate programs.

4. Build an online presence: Create a website, blog, or social media profile to establish your online presence and attract an audience.

5. Create valuable content: Produce high-quality content that educates, entertains, or solves problems for your target audience.

6. Promote affiliate products: Incorporate affiliate links or promo codes into your content and promote them through various marketing channels.

7. Track and optimize: Monitor your affiliate performance, track conversions, and optimize your marketing strategies to maximize your earnings.

Legal and Ethical Considerations

When engaging in affiliate marketing, it is essential to comply with legal and ethical guidelines:

1. Disclosure: Disclose your affiliate relationship to your audience by using clear and conspicuous disclosures in your content.

2. Truthfulness: Provide honest and accurate information about the products or services you promote.

3. Transparency: Clearly state any biases or conflicts of interest that may influence your recommendations.

4. Compliance: Adhere to applicable laws, regulations, and industry standards, such as the Federal Trade Commission (FTC) guidelines.

Affiliate marketing is a powerful marketing strategy that benefits both merchants and affiliates. It offers a flexible and scalable way to generate income by promoting products or services you believe in. By understanding the fundamentals of affiliate marketing and implementing effective strategies, you can build a successful affiliate business and achieve your financial goals.

CHAPTER 2

THE POWER OF TIKTOK FOR AFFILIATE MARKETING

TikTok is a popular social media platform that allows users to create and share short videos. With over 1 billion active users worldwide, TikTok has become a powerful tool for content creators, influencers, and businesses to reach a massive audience. Its unique algorithm and engaging features make it an ideal platform for affiliate marketing.

The Explosive Growth of TikTok

TikTok has experienced phenomenal growth since its launch in 2016. With over 1 billion monthly active users, it has become a dominant social media platform that appeals to various demographics, not just teenagers. This massive user base presents countless opportunities for affiliate marketers.

Why TikTok is the Perfect Platform for Affiliate Marketing: TikTok's short-form video content, addictive nature, and diverse audience make it an ideal platform for promoting affiliate products. Users are more likely to engage with entertaining and informative content, giving marketers a chance to showcase products creatively and effectively.

Why TikTok is Effective for Affiliate Marketing

TikTok offers several advantages that make it a powerful platform for affiliate marketing:

1. Massive user base: with millions of active users, TikTok provides a vast audience for the promotion of affiliate products or services.

2. Viral potential: TikTok's algorithm is designed to promote content that resonates with users, increasing the chances of your videos going viral and reaching a wider audience.

3. Authenticity and creativity: TikTok encourages users to be creative and authentic, allowing affiliates to showcase products in unique and engaging ways.

4. Short and snappy format: TikTok's short video format (15 to 60 seconds) is perfect for capturing attention and delivering concise promotional messages.

5. Trending challenges and hashtags: TikTok's trending challenges and hashtags provide opportunities for affiliates to participate and gain exposure.

6. Interactive features: TikTok offers various interactive features like duets, reactions, and comments, allowing

affiliates to engage with their audience and build a community.

7. Discoverability: TikTok's "for you" page showcases content based on user preferences, increasing the chances of your videos being discovered by new users.

Strategies for Affiliate Marketing on TikTok

To leverage the power of TikTok for affiliate marketing, consider the following strategies:

1. Choose the right niche: identify a niche that aligns with your interests and expertise, ensuring that there is an audience interested in the products or services you plan to promote.

2. Create engaging content: Use TikTok's creative tools, effects, and music to create visually appealing and entertaining videos that capture the attention of viewers.

3. Showcase products naturally: integrate affiliate products seamlessly into your content by demonstrating their benefits, sharing personal experiences, or providing valuable tips and recommendations.

4. Utilize trending challenges and hashtags: participate in popular challenges and use relevant hashtags to increase the visibility of your content and reach a wider audience.

5. Engage with your audience: respond to comments, collaborate with other TikTok creators, and encourage user-generated content to foster engagement and build a loyal following.

6. Provide value: offer valuable information, tips, or entertainment in your videos to establish yourself as a trusted authority in your niche and gain the trust of your audience.

7. Track and optimize: monitor the performance of your affiliate links, track conversions, and analyze the engagement metrics of your TikTok videos to optimize your strategies and maximize your earnings.

Legal and Ethical Considerations on TikTok

When using TikTok for affiliate marketing, it is crucial to adhere to legal and ethical guidelines:

1. Disclosure: clearly disclose your affiliate relationship in your videos or captions to ensure transparency with your audience.

2. Authenticity: only promote products or services that you genuinely believe in and have personally tested or researched.

3. Compliance: adhere to TikTok's community guidelines and any applicable laws or regulations regarding advertising and disclosure.

4. Respect intellectual property: avoid using copyrighted material without permission and give proper credit to creators when using their content.

Success Stories of Affiliate Marketing on TikTok

TikTok has witnessed numerous success stories in affiliate marketing. Influencers and content creators have been able to generate significant income by promoting affiliate products or services to their engaged TikTok audience. These success stories highlight the potential of TikTok as a lucrative platform for affiliate marketing.

The TikTok Algorithm: Understanding its Potential for Success

TikTok's algorithm focuses on user behavior, making it easier for content to go viral. By creating content that resonates with your target audience, you can reach a larger audience and increase your chances of success in affiliate marketing.

Actionable Steps for Chapter 2:

1. Create a TikTok account if you haven't already and familiarize yourself with the platform.
2. Analyze popular TikTok accounts in your niche to understand the type of content that resonates with your target audience.
3. Study the TikTok algorithm and identify best practices to increase the visibility of your content.

Remember, TikTok is a platform for users of all ages and backgrounds, providing ample opportunities for affiliate marketers to reach diverse audiences.

TikTok's immense popularity and unique features make it a powerful tool for affiliate marketing. By leveraging TikTok's massive user base, creative tools, and interactive features, affiliates can effectively promote products or services and generate income. However, it is essential to maintain authenticity, provide value, and comply with legal and ethical guidelines to build a successful affiliate marketing presence on TikTok.

CHOOSING THE RIGHT AFFILIATE MARKETING PROGRAM

Affiliate marketing programs are partnerships between merchants and affiliates, where affiliates promote the merchant's products or services and earn a commission for each sale or lead generated through their efforts. Choosing the right affiliate marketing program is crucial for the success of your affiliate marketing journey.

Factors to Consider When Choosing an Affiliate Marketing Program

When selecting an affiliate marketing program, consider the following factors:

1. Relevance to Your Niche: Choose an affiliate program that offers products or services relevant to your niche or target audience. Promoting products that align with your content and expertise will increase the chances of success.

2. Commission Structure: Evaluate the commission structure of the affiliate program. Look for programs that offer competitive commission rates and fair compensation for your efforts.

3. Cookie Duration: Cookie duration refers to the length of time a cookie (a small piece of data) is stored on a user's device after they click on your affiliate link. Longer cookie durations provide a higher chance of earning a commission if the user makes a purchase within that timeframe.

4. Payment Schedule: Consider the payment schedule of the affiliate program. Some programs pay monthly, while others have a longer payment cycle. Choose a program that aligns with your financial goals and cash flow requirements.

5. Affiliate Support: Look for programs that provide adequate support to affiliates. This may include access to marketing materials, dedicated affiliate managers, and timely responses to queries or concerns.

6. Reputation and Trustworthiness: Research the reputation and trustworthiness of the affiliate program and the merchant. Look for programs with a track record of timely payments, fair practices, and positive reviews from other affiliates.

7. Tracking and Reporting: Ensure that the affiliate program has a reliable tracking system in place to accurately track your referrals and conversions. Access to detailed reporting and

analytics will help you monitor your performance and optimize your strategies.

8. Affiliate Tools and Resources: Consider the availability of affiliate tools and resources provided by the program. These may include banners, product images, landing pages, and promotional materials that can enhance your marketing efforts.

9. Restrictions and Policies: Review the program's restrictions and policies, such as prohibited promotional methods, geographical limitations, or exclusions on certain products or services. Ensure that these align with your marketing strategies and target audience.

Researching and Evaluating Affiliate Marketing Programs

To choose the right affiliate marketing program, follow these steps:

1. Research: Conduct thorough research to identify affiliate programs that align with your niche and meet your criteria. Explore affiliate networks, merchant websites, and online forums to find suitable programs.

2. Read Reviews and Testimonials: Look for reviews and testimonials from other affiliates who have experience with the program. This can provide insights into the program's reputation, payment reliability, and overall satisfaction.

3. Analyze Program Details: Review the program's commission structure, cookie duration, payment schedule, and affiliate support. Compare these details across different programs to identify the most favorable options.

4. Consider Merchant Reputation: Research the reputation of the merchant associated with the affiliate program. Look for

merchants with a positive track record, quality products or services, and a strong brand presence.

5. Join Affiliate Forums and Communities: Engage with affiliate forums and communities to seek recommendations and insights from experienced affiliates. These platforms can provide valuable information and help you make informed decisions.

6. Reach Out to Affiliate Managers: Contact the affiliate managers of the programs you are interested in. Ask questions, clarify any doubts, and assess their responsiveness and willingness to support affiliates.

7. Test and Monitor Performance: Once you have chosen an affiliate program, start promoting the products or services and closely monitor your performance. Evaluate the program's effectiveness based on your conversions, earnings, and overall satisfaction.

Diversifying Affiliate Programs

Consider diversifying your affiliate programs to mitigate risks and maximize your earnings. By promoting products or services from multiple programs, you can cater to a broader audience, leverage different commission structures, and reduce dependency on a single program.

High-paying vs. High-converting Affiliate Programs

High-paying affiliate programs offer larger commissions but may have lower conversion rates, while high-converting programs pay lower commissions but convert more customers. Evaluate your goals and choose a program that balances both factors.

Top Affiliate Networks and Programs to Consider

Popular affiliate networks like Amazon Associates, ShareASale, and ClickBank offer a wide range of products and services. Research different networks and programs to find the best fit for your niche and audience.

Actionable Steps for Chapter 3:

1. List down factors that are important to you in an affiliate program.
2. Research various affiliate networks and programs to identify potential options.
3. Select an affiliate program that aligns with your niche, audience, and preferences.

Choosing the right affiliate marketing program is crucial for your success as an affiliate marketer. Consider factors such as relevance to your niche, commission structure, cookie duration, payment schedule, affiliate support, reputation, and tracking capabilities when evaluating programs. Thorough research, analysis, and monitoring will help you make informed decisions and optimize your affiliate marketing efforts. Remember to diversify your affiliate programs to expand your opportunities and minimize risks.

CHAPTER 4

CREATING ENGAGING TIKTOK CONTENT FOR AFFILIATE MARKETING

Creating engaging TikTok content is essential for successful affiliate marketing on the platform. TikTok's algorithm prioritizes content that resonates with users, making it crucial to capture their attention and deliver compelling promotional messages. This chapter will guide you through the process of creating engaging TikTok content for affiliate marketing.

Understanding Your Target Audience

Before creating TikTok content, it is crucial to understand your target audience. Consider their demographics, interests, preferences, and pain points. This understanding will help you tailor your content to their needs and increase the chances of engagement and conversions.

Tips for Producing Viral-worthy TikTok Videos

To create engaging TikTok content, focus on quality, storytelling, and entertainment value. Keep your videos short, visually appealing, and informative.

Leveraging TikTok's Creative Tools and Effects

TikTok offers a wide range of creative tools and effects that can enhance your content and make it more engaging. Experiment with features like filters, stickers, text overlays, transitions, and special effects to add visual appeal and captivate your audience.

Showcasing Products or Services Naturally

When promoting affiliate products or services on TikTok, it is essential to showcase them naturally within your content. Avoid being overly promotional or salesy, as this can turn off viewers. Instead, focus on demonstrating the benefits, sharing personal experiences, or providing valuable tips and recommendations related to the product or service.

Incorporating Storytelling Techniques

Storytelling is a powerful technique to engage and connect with your audience. Use storytelling elements in your TikTok content to create a narrative that resonates with viewers. This can involve sharing personal anecdotes, testimonials, or relatable scenarios that highlight the value of the affiliate product or service.

Utilizing Trending Challenges and Hashtags

TikTok is known for its trending challenges and hashtags. Participating in popular challenges and using relevant hashtags can increase the visibility of your content and attract a wider audience. Incorporate affiliate products or services creatively into these challenges, ensuring they align with the theme and purpose of the challenge.

Engaging with Your Audience

Engagement is key to building a loyal TikTok following and driving conversions. Respond to comments, ask questions, and encourage viewers to interact with your content. Engage with other TikTok creators by collaborating on duets or reactions, fostering a sense of community and increasing your reach.

Providing Value to Your Audience

To establish yourself as a trusted authority in your niche, provide value to your audience through your TikTok content.

Offer valuable information, tips, tutorials, or entertainment that aligns with their interests and needs. This will build trust and credibility, increasing the likelihood of viewers taking action on your affiliate promotions.

Optimizing Video Length and Captions

TikTok's short video format (15 to 60 seconds) requires concise and impactful content. Keep your videos engaging and to the point, capturing attention within the first few seconds. Use captions effectively to convey your message, as many viewers watch TikTok videos with the sound off.

Tracking Performance and Analyzing Metrics

Monitor the performance of your TikTok content to understand what resonates with your audience and drives conversions. Track metrics such as views, likes, shares, comments, and click-through rates on your affiliate links.

Analyze this data to optimize your content strategy and focus on what generates the best results.

Collaborating with Influencers and TikTok Creators

Consider collaborating with influencers or TikTok creators who have a similar target audience or niche. Collaborations can expand your reach, introduce your affiliate products or services to new audiences, and provide social proof. Ensure that the influencers align with your brand values and have an engaged following.

Staying Authentic and Transparent

Authenticity and transparency are crucial for building trust with your TikTok audience. Clearly disclose your affiliate relationship in your videos or captions to ensure transparency. Only promote products or services that you genuinely believe in and have personally tested or researched.

Experimenting and Iterating

TikTok is a dynamic platform, and trends change quickly. Experiment with different content formats, styles, and strategies to find what works best for your audience. Continuously iterate and optimize your content based on audience feedback and performance metrics.

Actionable Steps for Chapter 4:

1. Define your target audience and their preferences.
2. Develop a content strategy that caters to your audience's needs and interests.
3. Experiment with different video formats, storytelling techniques, and humor to make your content stand out.

Creating engaging TikTok content is essential for successful affiliate marketing on the platform. By understanding your target audience, leveraging TikTok's creative tools, showcasing products naturally, incorporating storytelling techniques, utilizing trending challenges and hashtags, engaging with your audience, providing value, and tracking performance, you can create compelling content that drives engagement and conversions. Stay authentic, transparent, and open to experimentation to maximize your success on TikTok as an affiliate marketer.

CHAPTER 5

OPTIMIZING YOUR TIKTOK PROFILE FOR AFFILIATE MARKETING SUCCESS

Optimizing your TikTok profile is crucial for affiliate marketing success on the platform. Your profile serves as a first impression for potential followers and can influence their decision to engage with your content and click on your affiliate links. This chapter will guide you through the process of optimizing your TikTok profile for affiliate marketing success.

Choose a Relevant Username

Select a username that is relevant to your niche or the products and services you plan to promote as an affiliate marketer. A username that aligns with your content will make it easier for users to find and remember your profile.

Craft a Compelling Bio

Your TikTok bio is an opportunity to introduce yourself and communicate your value proposition to potential followers. Craft a compelling bio that highlights your expertise, niche, and the benefits viewers can expect from following you. Include relevant keywords and hashtags to improve discoverability.

Use a High-Quality Profile Picture

Choose a high-quality profile picture that represents your
brand or personal identity. A clear and visually appealing
profile picture will make your profile more professional and
trustworthy.

Add Links to Your Affiliate Websites or Landing Pages

TikTok allows you to add one clickable link in your profile.
Utilize this feature by adding a link to your affiliate website or
landing page. Ensure that the link is relevant to your content
and leads to a page where users can learn more or make a
purchase.

Highlight Your Affiliate Partnerships

If you have established affiliate partnerships with specific
brands or companies, consider mentioning them in your
profile. This can build credibility and trust with your audience,

as they will see that you have established relationships with reputable brands.

Showcase Your Best TikTok Content

Feature your best TikTok content in your profile. Choose videos that have performed well in terms of views, likes, and engagement. This will give new visitors a taste of your content and encourage them to explore further.

Utilize TikTok's Featured Video Slot

TikTok allows you to pin a video to the top of your profile as a featured video. Take advantage of this feature by selecting a video that showcases your affiliate promotions or represents your brand effectively. This will ensure that new visitors see your most important content right away.

Engage with Your TikTok Community

Engagement is key to building a loyal following on TikTok. Respond to comments, engage with other creators, and encourage user-generated content. This will foster a sense of community and make your profile more appealing to potential followers.

Consistency in Posting

Consistency is crucial on TikTok. Develop a posting schedule and stick to it. Regularly uploading new content will keep your profile active and increase your chances of reaching a wider audience.

Collaborate with Influencers and TikTok Creators

Collaborating with influencers or TikTok creators in your niche can help you expand your reach and gain exposure to new audiences. Seek out collaboration opportunities that align with your brand and affiliate promotions.

Monitor and Analyze Profile Metrics

TikTok provides insights and analytics about your profile's performance. Monitor metrics such as follower growth, video views, engagement rates, and link clicks. Analyze this data to understand what content resonates with your audience and optimize your profile strategy accordingly.

Stay Authentic and Transparent

Authenticity and transparency are crucial for building trust with your TikTok audience. Clearly disclose your affiliate relationships in your videos or captions to ensure transparency. Only promote products or services that you genuinely believe in and have personally tested or researched.

Actionable Steps for Chapter 5:

1. Optimize your TikTok profile with a professional picture and keyword-rich bio.

2. Set up a link in your bio that directs users to your affiliate offers or landing pages.

3. Create content that integrates your affiliate offers naturally and provides value to your audience.

Optimizing your TikTok profile is essential for affiliate marketing success on the platform. By choosing a relevant username, crafting a compelling bio, using a high-quality profile picture, adding links to your affiliate websites or landing pages, highlighting your affiliate partnerships, showcasing your best TikTok content, utilizing TikTok's featured video slot, engaging with your community, maintaining consistency in posting, collaborating with influencers, monitoring profile metrics, and staying authentic and transparent, you can create a profile that attracts followers and drives conversions. Remember to regularly evaluate and optimize your profile strategy to maximize your success as an affiliate marketer on TikTok.

CHAPTER 6

LEVERAGING TIKTOK HASHTAGS AND TRENDS FOR MAXIMUM EXPOSURE

TikTok is known for its viral hashtags and trends that capture the attention of millions of users. As an affiliate marketer, leveraging these hashtags and trends can significantly boost your visibility, engagement, and ultimately, your affiliate marketing success. This chapter will guide you through the process of effectively using TikTok hashtags and trends for affiliate marketing.

Understanding TikTok Hashtags

Hashtags on TikTok are keywords or phrases preceded by the "#" symbol. They categorize and organize content, making it easier for users to discover videos related to specific topics. By using relevant hashtags, you can increase the visibility of your content and attract a wider audience.

Researching Trending Hashtags

Stay up to date with the latest trending hashtags on TikTok. Explore the Discover page, the For You page, and the Explore tab to identify popular hashtags related to your niche or the products and services you are promoting. Researching trending hashtags will help you align your content with what is currently popular and increase your chances of reaching a larger audience.

Using Niche-Specific Hashtags

In addition to trending hashtags, incorporate niche-specific hashtags into your content. These hashtags are more targeted and cater to a specific audience interested in your niche or the products and services you are promoting. Using niche-specific hashtags will help you attract a relevant audience that is more likely to engage with your content and convert.

Creating Branded Hashtags

Consider creating your own branded hashtags to establish a unique identity and encourage user-generated content. Branded hashtags can be related to your brand, your affiliate promotions, or a specific campaign. Encourage your followers to use your branded hashtags in their own videos, creating a sense of community and increasing brand visibility.

Participating in TikTok Challenges

TikTok challenges are popular trends that encourage users to create and share videos following a specific theme or concept. Participating in relevant challenges can significantly increase your visibility and engagement. Incorporate your affiliate promotions creatively into challenge videos, ensuring they align with the theme and purpose of the challenge.

Incorporating Hashtags in Captions and Comments

When using hashtags on TikTok, incorporate them strategically in your video captions and comments. Use a mix of popular and niche-specific hashtags to maximize your reach. Avoid using too many hashtags in a single caption, as it can make your content appear spammy. Instead, focus on using a few relevant hashtags that accurately represent your content.

Engaging with Hashtag Communities

Engage with the communities formed around popular hashtags related to your niche or affiliate promotions. Like, comment, and share videos that use these hashtags to increase your visibility and build connections with other TikTok creators and potential followers. Engaging with hashtag communities will help you establish yourself as an active and valuable member of the TikTok community.

Tracking Hashtag Performance

Monitor the performance of the hashtags you use in your TikTok content. Pay attention to metrics such as views, likes, shares, and comments on videos that include specific hashtags. Analyze this data to understand which hashtags generate the most engagement and adjust your hashtag strategy accordingly.

Staying Relevant and Adapting to Trends

TikTok trends and hashtags evolve quickly. Stay updated with the latest trends and adapt your content strategy accordingly. Monitor the For You page, follow relevant creators, and engage with the TikTok community to stay in tune with what is popular. By staying relevant and adapting to trends, you can maximize your visibility and engagement.

Collaborating with TikTok Creators and Influencers

Consider collaborating with TikTok creators or influencers who have a significant following and are known for participating in trending challenges or using popular hashtags. Collaborations can help you tap into their audience and increase your reach. Ensure that the creators align with your brand values and have an engaged following.

Actionable Steps for Chapter 6:

1. Research popular and trending hashtags relevant to your niche.

2. Incorporate trending music into your videos with low volume.
3. Study successful content and find ways to make it better or more engaging.

Leveraging TikTok hashtags and trends is a powerful strategy for affiliate marketing success on the platform. By understanding TikTok hashtags, researching trending and niche-specific hashtags, creating branded hashtags, participating in challenges, incorporating hashtags strategically, engaging with hashtag communities, tracking hashtag performance, staying relevant, adapting to trends, and collaborating with TikTok creators and influencers, you can significantly increase your visibility, engagement, and conversions. Remember to continuously monitor and optimize your hashtag strategy to stay ahead of the game and maximize your success as an affiliate marketer on TikTok.

CHAPTER 7

CONSISTENCY IS KEY IN AFFILIATE MARKETING

Consistency is a fundamental principle that plays a crucial role in the success of affiliate marketing. It involves maintaining a regular and reliable presence in your marketing efforts, consistently delivering valuable content, and consistently engaging with your audience. This chapter will explore the importance of consistency in affiliate marketing and provide strategies for implementing it effectively.

Building Trust and Credibility

Consistency builds trust and credibility with your audience. When you consistently show up and deliver valuable content, your audience begins to rely on you as a reliable source of information and recommendations. This trust and credibility are essential for driving conversions and establishing long-term relationships with your audience.

Establishing Brand Identity

Consistency in your marketing efforts helps establish a strong brand identity. By consistently presenting your brand's values, messaging, and visual elements, you create a recognizable and memorable brand. This consistency allows your audience to easily identify and connect with your brand, increasing brand loyalty and affinity.

Developing a Content Schedule

Creating a content schedule is a key aspect of maintaining consistency in affiliate marketing. Plan and organize your content in advance, ensuring a regular flow of valuable and engaging content for your audience. A content schedule helps you stay organized, ensures a consistent presence, and allows you to plan your affiliate promotions strategically.

Providing Value on a Regular Basis

Consistency involves consistently providing value to your audience. Regularly share informative, educational, or entertaining content that aligns with your niche and the interests of your audience. This consistent value delivery builds trust, keeps your audience engaged, and positions you as an authority in your field.

Engaging with Your Audience

Consistency extends beyond content creation; it also applies to engaging with your audience. Respond to comments, messages, and inquiries in a timely manner. Show genuine interest in your audience's feedback and questions. Consistent engagement fosters a sense of community and strengthens the relationship between you and your audience.

Leveraging Multiple Marketing Channels

Consistency should extend across multiple marketing channels. While TikTok may be your primary platform, consider leveraging other channels such as Instagram, YouTube, or a blog to reach a wider audience. Maintain a consistent brand presence and messaging across all channels to reinforce your brand identity and increase your reach.

Tracking and Analyzing Performance

Consistency allows you to track and analyze the performance of your affiliate marketing efforts more effectively. By consistently monitoring metrics such as click-through rates, conversion rates, and engagement rates, you can identify patterns, optimize your strategies, and make data-driven decisions to improve your results.

Adapting and Evolving

Consistency does not mean sticking to the same strategies indefinitely. It also involves adapting and evolving your approach based on feedback, market trends, and audience preferences. Continuously evaluate your performance, experiment with new ideas, and refine your strategies to stay relevant and meet the evolving needs of your audience.

Overcoming Challenges and Staying Motivated

Consistency can be challenging, especially when faced with obstacles or setbacks. It is important to stay motivated and overcome these challenges. Set realistic goals, celebrate small wins, seek support from like-minded individuals or communities, and remind yourself of the long-term benefits that consistency brings to your affiliate marketing success.

Collaboration and Networking

Collaborating with other affiliate marketers or influencers in your niche can help you maintain consistency and expand your reach. By partnering with others, you can share resources, cross-promote each other's content, and tap into new audiences. Collaboration and networking provide opportunities for growth and help you stay consistent in your marketing efforts.

Action Steps for Chapter 7:

1. Establish your brand identity through consistency.

2. Develop a content schedule. Plan the work and stay organized.

3. Engage with your audience. Set aside time daily to respond to comments and inquiries.

4. Collaborate with other affiliate marketers to expand your reach. Be creative, share resources, and cross-promote.

Consistency is a key principle in affiliate marketing that builds trust, establishes brand identity, and drives long-term success. By consistently delivering valuable content, engaging with your audience, leveraging multiple marketing channels, tracking performance, adapting to changes, overcoming challenges, and collaborating with others, you can maintain a consistent presence and maximize your affiliate marketing results. Remember, consistency is not a one-time effort but an ongoing commitment that will yield significant rewards in the

long run.

CHAPTER 8

TRACKING AND ANALYZING YOUR AFFILIATE MARKETING PERFORMANCE

Tracking and analyzing your affiliate marketing performance is essential for understanding the effectiveness of your strategies, optimizing your campaigns, and maximizing your results. This chapter will guide you through the process of tracking and analyzing your affiliate marketing performance to make data-driven decisions and improve your overall success.

Setting Clear Goals and Objectives

Before you start tracking and analyzing your affiliate marketing performance, it's important to set clear goals and objectives. Define what you want to achieve with your affiliate marketing efforts, whether it's increasing conversions, driving more traffic, or boosting revenue. Clear goals will provide a benchmark for measuring your performance.

Tracking Affiliate Links and Conversions

One of the key aspects of tracking your affiliate marketing performance is monitoring the performance of your affiliate links and conversions. Use tracking tools provided by your affiliate network or third-party tracking software to track clicks, conversions, and sales generated through your affiliate links. This data will help you understand which campaigns and strategies are driving the most conversions.

Analyzing Traffic Sources

Analyze the sources of traffic that are driving visitors to your affiliate links. Use analytics tools like Google Analytics to identify the channels, websites, or social media platforms that are sending the most traffic. This information will help you focus your efforts on the most effective traffic sources and optimize your marketing strategies accordingly.

8.5 Monitoring Conversion Rates

Conversion rates are a critical metric to track and analyze in affiliate marketing. Calculate your conversion rate by dividing the number of conversions by the number of clicks on your affiliate links. Monitor your conversion rates over time to identify trends and patterns. A low conversion rate may indicate a need to optimize your landing pages, improve your call-to-action, or refine your targeting.

Evaluating Revenue and Earnings

Tracking your revenue and earnings is crucial for understanding the financial impact of your affiliate marketing efforts. Monitor the revenue generated from your affiliate campaigns and calculate your earnings by subtracting any costs or fees associated with your affiliate program. Analyze your revenue and earnings to determine the profitability of your campaigns and make informed decisions about resource allocation.

Analyzing Audience Engagement

Engagement metrics provide insights into how your audience is interacting with your affiliate marketing content. Monitor metrics such as likes, comments, shares, and click-through rates to gauge audience engagement. Analyze which types of content or campaigns are generating the most engagement and tailor your strategies accordingly.

A/B Testing and Experimentation

A/B testing involves comparing two versions of a campaign or landing page to determine which performs better. Experiment with different elements such as headlines, visuals, calls-to-action, or promotional offers to see which variations yield higher conversions. A/B testing allows you to optimize your campaigns based on data and continuously improve your affiliate marketing performance.

Analyzing Return on Investment (ROI)

Calculating your return on investment (ROI) is crucial for understanding the profitability of your affiliate marketing efforts. Compare the revenue generated from your campaigns to the costs incurred, including advertising expenses, affiliate program fees, and any other associated costs. Analyzing your ROI will help you identify the most profitable campaigns and allocate your resources effectively.

Utilizing Analytics Tools and Reports

Leverage analytics tools and reports provided by your affiliate network, tracking software, or third-party platforms to gain deeper insights into your affiliate marketing performance. These tools can provide detailed data on clicks, conversions, revenue, audience demographics, and more. Utilize these tools to track your progress, identify trends, and make data-driven decisions.

Staying Up to Date with Industry Trends

Stay informed about the latest industry trends and best practices in affiliate marketing. Follow industry blogs, attend webinars, and participate in forums or communities to stay updated. By staying current with industry trends, you can adapt your strategies, leverage new opportunities, and stay ahead of the competition.

Continuous Optimization and Improvement

Tracking and analyzing your affiliate marketing performance is an ongoing process. Continuously monitor your metrics, identify areas for improvement, and optimize your campaigns based on data-driven insights. Regularly evaluate your strategies, experiment with new approaches, and refine your tactics to maximize your affiliate marketing success.

Actionable Steps for Chapter 8:

1. Regularly track and analyze key metrics to assess your content's performance.
2. Use analytics tools to gain insights and refine your content strategy.
3. Conduct split tests and optimize your content based on the results.

4. Stay persistent and be open to trying new affiliate programs if needed.

Tracking and analyzing your affiliate marketing performance is crucial for understanding the effectiveness of your strategies, optimizing your campaigns, and maximizing your results. By setting clear goals, tracking affiliate links and conversions, analyzing traffic sources, monitoring conversion rates, evaluating revenue and earnings, analyzing audience engagement, conducting A/B testing, calculating ROI, utilizing analytics tools, staying up to date with industry trends, and continuously optimizing and improving, you can make data-driven decisions and achieve greater success in your affiliate marketing efforts. Remember, tracking and analysis are ongoing processes that require regular attention and adjustment to stay ahead in the dynamic world of affiliate marketing.

The Affiliate Marketing Revolution: An Ironclad Blueprint for Results

CHAPTER 9

SCALING AND DIVERSIFYING IN AFFILIATE MARKETING

Scaling and diversifying your affiliate marketing efforts are essential strategies for expanding your reach, increasing your revenue, and achieving long-term success. This chapter will explore the importance of scaling and diversifying in affiliate marketing and provide strategies for implementing these strategies effectively.

Understanding Scaling in Affiliate Marketing

Scaling in affiliate marketing refers to the process of increasing the volume and reach of your campaigns to generate more traffic, conversions, and revenue. Scaling allows you to leverage successful campaigns and strategies to maximize your results and grow your affiliate business.

Analyzing Successful Campaigns

To scale your affiliate marketing efforts, analyze your successful campaigns to identify patterns and strategies that have yielded positive results. Look for campaigns that have generated high conversions, revenue, or engagement. Analyze the elements that contributed to their success, such as the targeting, messaging, visuals, or promotional offers.

Replicating Successful Campaigns

Once you have identified successful campaigns, replicate them by creating similar campaigns with slight variations. Use the same targeting parameters, messaging, and promotional offers, but adapt them to different audiences or platforms. Replicating successful campaigns allows you to leverage proven strategies and increase your chances of success.

Expanding to New Platforms

Scaling in affiliate marketing involves expanding your presence to new platforms. If you have been successful on one platform, consider diversifying your efforts by exploring other platforms such as Instagram, YouTube, Pinterest, or a blog. Each platform has its own unique audience and engagement opportunities, allowing you to reach a wider audience and diversify your traffic sources.

Leveraging Automation and Tools

To scale your affiliate marketing efforts efficiently, leverage automation and tools. Use automation tools to streamline repetitive tasks such as content scheduling, social media posting, or email marketing. Invest in tracking and analytics tools to monitor your campaigns' performance and make data-driven decisions. These tools will save you time and allow you to focus on scaling your efforts.

Building a Team or Outsourcing

As your affiliate marketing business grows, consider building a team or outsourcing certain tasks to experts. Hiring team members or outsourcing tasks such as content creation, graphic design, or campaign management can help you scale your efforts more effectively. Delegating responsibilities allows you to focus on strategic planning and scaling your business.

Diversifying Affiliate Programs and Networks

Diversifying your affiliate programs and networks is crucial for mitigating risks and expanding your revenue streams. Join multiple affiliate programs and networks that align with your niche or target audience. This diversification ensures that you are not solely reliant on one program or network and allows you to tap into different product offerings and commission structures.

Exploring New Niches and Products

Diversification in affiliate marketing involves exploring new niches and products. Research and identify complementary niches or related products that align with your audience's interests. By expanding into new niches or promoting different products, you can reach a broader audience and diversify your revenue sources.

Testing and Experimentation

Scaling and diversifying in affiliate marketing require continuous testing and experimentation. Test different strategies, platforms, promotional offers, or messaging to identify what works best for your audience. Experimentation allows you to discover new opportunities, optimize your campaigns, and adapt to changing market trends.

Monitoring and Analyzing Performance

As you scale and diversify your affiliate marketing efforts, it's crucial to monitor and analyze the performance of your campaigns. Continuously track metrics such as clicks, conversions, revenue, and engagement to understand the effectiveness of your strategies. Analyze the data to identify areas for improvement, optimize your campaigns, and make informed decisions.

Adapting and Evolving

Scaling and diversifying in affiliate marketing requires adaptability and a willingness to evolve. Stay updated with industry trends, consumer behavior, and changes in the affiliate marketing landscape. Continuously evaluate your strategies, experiment with new approaches, and adapt your tactics to stay ahead of the competition and maximize your results.

Actionable Steps for Chapter 9:

1. Focus on building a loyal TikTok following by engaging with your audience and posting consistently.
2. Diversify your affiliate marketing portfolio by promoting a variety of products and services.
3. Create accounts on other social media platforms and integrate affiliate marketing strategies across these channels.

Scaling and diversifying in affiliate marketing are essential strategies for expanding your reach, increasing your revenue, and achieving long-term success. By analyzing successful campaigns, replicating strategies, expanding to new platforms, leveraging automation and tools, building a team or outsourcing, diversifying affiliate programs and networks, exploring new niches and products, testing and experimenting, monitoring and analyzing performance, and adapting and evolving, you can scale and diversify your affiliate marketing efforts effectively. Remember, scaling and diversifying require continuous effort, strategic planning, and a willingness to adapt to the ever-changing affiliate marketing landscape.

CHAPTER 10

USING TIKTOK ADS FOR AFFILIATE MARKETING

TikTok has emerged as one of the fastest-growing social media platforms, offering a unique opportunity for affiliate marketers to reach a large and engaged audience. This chapter will explore the benefits of using TikTok Ads for affiliate marketing and provide strategies for effectively leveraging this platform to drive conversions and increase revenue.

Understanding TikTok's Audience and Reach

TikTok boasts a massive user base, particularly among younger demographics. Understanding the platform's audience and reach is crucial for successful affiliate marketing. TikTok's users are highly engaged and receptive to creative and entertaining content, making it an ideal platform for promoting affiliate products and generating conversions.

Setting Up a TikTok Ads Account

To start using TikTok Ads for affiliate marketing, you need to set up a TikTok Ads account. Visit the TikTok Ads Manager website and follow the registration process. Once your account is set up, you can create and manage your ad campaigns directly within the TikTok Ads Manager platform.

Defining Your Target Audience

Before creating TikTok ad campaigns, it's important to define your target audience. Consider the demographics, interests, and behaviors of your ideal customers. TikTok offers various targeting options, including age, gender, location, interests, and more. By defining your target audience, you can create more effective and relevant ad campaigns.

Choosing the Right Ad Format

TikTok offers several ad formats to choose from, each with its unique features and benefits. The available ad formats include in-feed ads, branded effects, branded hashtag challenges, and top-view ads. Consider your campaign goals, target audience, and the type of content that resonates best with your audience when selecting the right ad format for your affiliate marketing campaigns.

Creating Compelling Ad Content

Creating compelling ad content is crucial for capturing the attention of TikTok users and driving conversions. TikTok is a platform known for its creative and entertaining content, so focuses on creating visually appealing and engaging ads. Use high-quality visuals, catchy captions, and compelling calls to action to encourage users to take action and click on your affiliate links.

Incorporating Influencer Marketing

Influencer marketing is a powerful strategy to leverage on TikTok. Collaborating with influencers who have a large and engaged following can help you reach a wider audience and build trust with potential customers. Identify influencers in your niche and negotiate partnerships where they promote your affiliate products in their TikTok content.

Tracking and Analyzing Campaign Performance

Tracking and analyzing the performance of your TikTok ad campaigns is essential for optimizing your strategies and maximizing your results. Utilize the analytics tools provided by TikTok Ads Manager to monitor metrics such as impressions, clicks, conversions, and engagement rates. Analyze the data to identify trends, optimize your campaigns, and make data-driven decisions.

Testing and Iterating

Testing and iterating your TikTok ad campaigns is crucial for refining your strategies and improving your results. Experiment with different ad formats, targeting options, visuals, captions, and calls-to-action to identify what resonates best with your audience. Continuously test and iterate your campaigns based on the data and feedback you receive.

Compliance with TikTok's Advertising Policies

When using TikTok Ads for affiliate marketing, it's important to comply with TikTok's advertising policies. Familiarize yourself with the platform's guidelines and ensure that your ad content adheres to their policies. Failure to comply with these policies can result in your ads being rejected or your account being suspended.

Building Relationships with TikTok Users

Building relationships with TikTok users is crucial for long-term success in affiliate marketing. Engage with users who interact with your ads by responding to comments, messages, and inquiries. Show genuine interest in their feedback and questions. Building relationships fosters trust and loyalty, increasing the likelihood of conversions and repeat customers.

Scaling and Optimizing Your TikTok Ad Campaigns

As you gain insights and experience with TikTok Ads, consider scaling and optimizing your campaigns. Increase your ad spend on successful campaigns, expand your targeting options, and explore new ad formats. Continuously monitor and analyze the performance of your campaigns to identify areas for improvement and make data-driven decisions.

Using TikTok Ads for affiliate marketing offers a unique opportunity to reach a large and engaged audience. By setting up a TikTok Ads account, defining your target audience, choosing the right ad format, creating compelling ad content, incorporating influencer marketing, tracking and analyzing campaign performance, testing and iterating, complying with TikTok's advertising policies, building relationships with TikTok users, and scaling and optimizing your campaigns, you can effectively leverage TikTok Ads to drive conversions and increase revenue in your affiliate marketing efforts. Remember, TikTok is a dynamic platform, so stay updated with the latest trends and best practices to stay ahead of the competition and maximize your results.

www.inspireinkpublishing.com

www.ingramcontent.com/pod-product-compliance
Lightning Source LLC
Chambersburg PA
CBHW050046260726
48658CB00005B/1797